OTHER PSALMS

PREVIOUS WINNERS OF THE VASSAR MILLER PRIZE
IN POETRY

Scott Cairns, Founding Editor
John Poch, Series Editor

Partial Eclipse by Tony Sanders
Selected by Richard Howard

Delirium by Barbara Hamby
Selected by Cynthia Macdonald

The Sublime by Jonathan Holden
Selected by Yusef Komunyakaa

American Crawl by Paul Allen
Selected by Sydney Lea

Soul Data by Mark Svenvold
Selected by Heather McHugh

Moving & St rage by Kathy Fagan
Selected by T. R. Hummer

A Protocol for Touch
by Constance Merritt
Selected by Eleanor Wilner

The Perseids by Karen Holmberg
Selected by Sherod Santos

The Self as Constellation
by Jeanine Hathaway
Selected by Madeline DeFrees

Bene-Dictions by Rush Rankin
Selected by Rosanna Warren

Losing and Finding by Karen Fiser
Selected by Lynne McMahon

The Black Beach by J. T. Barbarese
Selected by Andrew Hudgins

re-entry by Michael White
Selected by Paul Mariani

The Next Settlement
by Michael Robins
Selected by Anne Winters

Mister Martini by Richard Carr
Selected by Naomi Shihab Nye

Ohio Violence by Alison Stine
Selected by Eric Pankey

Stray Home by Amy M. Clark
Selected by Beth Ann Fennelly

Circles Where the Head Should Be
by Caki Wilkinson
Selected by J. D. McClatchy

Death of a Ventriloquist
by Gibson Fay-LeBlanc
Selected by Lisa Russ Spaar

Club Icarus by Matt W. Miller
Selected by Major Jackson

In the Permanent Collection by
Stefanie Wortman
Selected by Chad Davidson

OTHER PSALMS

JORDAN WINDHOLZ

WINNER 2014 VASSAR MILLER PRIZE IN POETRY

University of North Texas Press, Denton, Texas

10 9 8 7 6 5 4 3 2 1

Permissions:
University of North Texas Press
1155 Union Circle #311336
Denton, TX 76203-5017

The paper used in this book meets the minimum requirements of the American National Standard for Permanence of Paper for Printed Library Materials, z39.48.1984. Binding materials have been chosen for durability.

Windholz, Jordan, 1982–
  [Poems. Selections]
  Other psalms / poems by Jordan Windholz.—Edition: first
      pages cm—(Number 22 in the Vassar Miller prize in poetry series)
  Vassar Miller Prize in Poetry, 2014.
      ISBN 978-1-57441-600-8 (pbk. : alk. paper)—ISBN 978-1-57441-608-4 (ebook)
  I. Title. II. Series: Vassar Miller prize in poetry series ; no. 22.
  PS3623.I599A6 2015
  811'.6—dc23
                                    2014038862

Other Psalms is Number 22 in the Vassar Miller Prize in Poetry Series

The electronic edition of this book was made possible by the support of the Vick Family Foundation.

A confession: I recall a husband must return on
his shield that the psalmist might sing. I recall
the prophet, his parable slung like a stone.

CONTENTS

Contents

ACKNOWLEDGMENTS

All poetry is a kind of collaboration, and I have had the good fortune of knowing wise and generous collaborators. I would not even be a poet without Matthew Roth's early and continued support of my work. You were my first teacher. You introduced me to Frost. You introduced me to O'Hara. That is too much debt for one life. Because of her commitment to the communities poems make, Elizabeth Robinson is the best kind of poet a poet can learn from. I am thankful that I am one of the many she has mentored. You saw me as a poet before I did; without your original faith, this book would not be. Julie Carr taught me how to trust my ear. What semblance of craft or discipline I have is a result of your example and teaching. Thank you. Ruth Ellen Kocher taught me to love the beautiful and to earn each line I longed to keep. I hope these poems, some of them, have earned your admiration.

These poems also benefited from generous reading and rereading by great poets I am thankful to call friends: Michael Flatt, J. Michael Martinez, and James Belflower. And to Rivers and Lucas, for their willingness to read and to listen.

Thank you Averill Curdy for giving this collection a chance.

Thank you to all at UNT Press who have worked so diligently to bring this book to publication, but a special thank you to Karen DeVinney, who shepherded me through the publication process.

Thank you Mom, Dad, Rachel, and Colby. And Erin, what can I say that is not already born of your love for me? You are the breath that buoys my every word.

I am also grateful to those editors of the following journals in which some of these poems first appeared, sometimes with alternate titles:

32poems: "Gospel," "The Shepherd's Song," and "Bestiary"

American Letters & Commentary: "Fable"

Barrow Street: "The Parable's Psalm"

Best New Poets 2007: "The Psalm's Parable"

Bravado (New Zealand): "The Talk"

Diner: "(psalm), *From the retina we extract the face*"

Drunken Boat: "Invocation" and "Ruminant"

Eleven Eleven: "Parable"

New American Writing: "The Transfiguration"

OmniVerse: "(psalm), *something like grace*"

Pebble Lake Review: "Of Revelation"

Quarterly West: "Myth"

Sou'wester: "Evangel"

SpringGun: selections from "Other Psalms"

But as for now, what happens is this.
We use whatever appropriate symbols
we can for the things of God.

—Pseudo-Dionysius

INVOCATION

But vastness blurs and time beats level
   —G. M. Hopkins

  hasten / the sky's
      frayed clusters
 stop my eye against
      the blue / there
 its pearled and pulleyed
      light / the fettered
 song in cloud's throttled
      crack / roils the lake's
 stilled silts / crest
      and crash of waves throw
 the bank in / throes
      of scattered stones
 against the leaf / quakes
 the clash
      I hear / the forest
 timber splinter branches
 break and roots
      uproot / the sight cleaves
 the breath's
      hitched / winds bend
 the boughs
      in gale's howl / the chime
 of color the floret cloaks is
      no sound / I know
 or see / these jointed
      sights disjointed even
 salvage them
      as I sing / hasten

1

PARABLE

First the inquiry, then charity. A listener is told *you come across one injured, beaten, robbed,* or *you scour your house for the gems of mollusks.* Look at the lilies, look at the sparrows. Here and gone. Here and gone. It's a ceremony of flesh: *the body a vase of embers, the skull a tabernacle.* Its listener parses air from error, sense from sensation. What's spoken reminds the body the voice is not yet its saint. Then the thought: it should crack the crown, emerge from the temple a goddess. Exiled into a strange landscape, it would stretch out under a placid sky. That sky an abrasion of burnt atmosphere. That sky a morality woven of accidents.

MYTH

The our before was and is
shall will out our now. All of

this this the said said. One God so
like time, before made these two, only

so little, and down it all came.
Not on time, but very like

God, if there were her and him, and he
and she like God, down came time,

the be into God, and out of the, the. Other
I, she, and other you, he. Their

there came down after us, these
came down after us. Them, all this time

before after, from God like God
over two, those little down came.

(PSALM)

From the retina we extract the face
    of the man in the moon, stuff our

pockets with photographs of his
    limbic gesticulation, his mouth

awed by the black dregs at a system's
    edge. With an ear to the firmament

the stars transmute a tinny voice, a
    phonograph's muffled static undoes

the ligature of a sphere's music. It's
    much easier to wrap in night's blanket,

warmed by its cliché, much safer to say,
    beyond a distance, another distance, beneath

a mystery, another mystery. From our own
    rib cages we construct deities shrouded

with the efficacy of prime numbers, or we
    extract our own voices, wads of wool

and spittle. In the end, dear lord, from
    a fallow hunger we remove a gaunt

appellation, something closer to
    you, a sound with a hole in it,

an etiolated luster sunken into its lack.

A NECESSARY ANGEL
RECALLS UNEARTHING ITS
TERRESTRIAL EXISTENCE

For though I knew the archives
sealed the former lives

of those who pledged themselves
to desert crypts or to the tops

of pillars, beholden to nothing
but what nothing offers, I

was surprised to find a life
I never knew I lived in

those desiccated texts.
Stripped of name, I saw

myself as if in a history
of sudden futures. Though devoted,

I was pagan. I invented gods,
carved them from the tusks

of butchered mammoths.
I made them tinier than

the bones of a sparrow's neck,
of the ear that interprets

its chitter as song. Though
I understood the necessity

of deities, I had no use
for sanctums, assumed

pockets would suffice.
When I walked, I'd thumb

their faces smooth, rub the skin's
oil over their ivory scowls

until their visages resembled
the blank stare of a proper

holiness. I had no mind
for prayer, or if I had, I had

not yet found an adequate
method for shaping words

into the winged things that
circle the incensed thrones

like seraphim, that sing the
supplications of those whose

lives necessitate the real heaven
where gods soundly sleep.

THE PSALM'S PARABLE

Suppose the chest unclasps
    like an ancient tome, its tales
loosed from the hermetic press

      of page upon page. Suppose the prose
it reveals resembles the anatomy
      of auks, the migratory patterns of certain

pacific starfish that court the currents around
      sandbars and coral. Or suppose the chest
is a salt-worn residence, its planks

      warped and gouged with pests, its floors
littered with legends and ballads. Suppose one
      of them speaks of journey and wandering

as stemming from the same seed. Imagine
      the tangle as metaphor is made. Outside the doors
of books or home, in wilderness, imagine

      a bush crowded with rose hips, a glistered gnarl,
itself a collapse of burning and speaking.

EPIPHANY

one emerald hummingbird hovers—

a local euphoria—a thrum

of sentences burled in verbs—the engine of

its heart—the mechanic flit and pat—sugared—

red—the sound of it—quietly quietly

and yes and yes and yes.

2

THE NOMADS

We had forgotten to build the altar,
which was a problem, considering we had
already slit the throats of the unblemished

firstborns of the herd, had already split
the doves and pigeons and excavated
their delicate shrines of song, removed

their organs to form more adequate hollows
for our penitence. It was Tuesday,
or so we hoped, having extended

the sanctity of our Sabbath too long.
Even the priests, it seemed, had misplaced
their ululations, for if they hadn't, why

disrobe, flagellate, and shower themselves
with ash beyond the allotted time?
The sacred oils too had soured, their aromas

curdled as they folded upon themselves
too rich. It also seemed that the star charts
plotted by our ancestors confused

the cardinal directions, a mistake we
realized too late. Our wandering had become
so routine it no longer sustained

the steeped meaning of story; the towers
of fire and cloud had spun the desert sand
into a tomorrow we could no longer

long for, but anyway, those guides had
forsaken us some time ago. Weeks earlier,
we stumbled upon an oasis, but found fruit

too sweet, waters too bright, and hominids
without language but dexterous with flinty spears.
They stole our ephods, two of our older scrolls,

as well as the herbs used to initiate trances,
without which we could not access
the curtained realms of angelic heraldry.

Our prophet had gnawed off his own tongue
at the sight of such loss, and his body convulsed
from the withdrawal of their bitter potency.

But we continued. It was as if each day's
horizon had become a mirror of our exodus,
the idea of that distance the holy ground

where we would come face to face with
our reflections fully realized, and understand
ourselves as the nomads we knew we were.

Though we had abandoned our calendars
some time ago, another night fell upon us.
The burnished scent of spent blood

suffused the camp. We tried to read what little
scriptures we had, but found them devoid of
pneuma. It wasn't as if our texts were now

inscrutable, but that any interpretation we
ventured clicked into inevitable prescription.
If a psalm, the music raveled within unspooled

too easily, and the air that bore its harmonies
hung over us like a humid cloth that seemed
a costume we had always been fated to wear.

THE INCARNATION

a certain threnody shivers the stereocilia

filling language with less

precious metals or filing it into the composite dust
    of stones

one cannot avoid the voice that haunts the word

within the supplication there is a pronoun that is a cup
    of cinder

one that is a porcelain doll

there always exists the desire to speak

despite speech's occlusion

the said difficult to see through

there rests the insistence of margins

there remains the hope for more exquisite manifestation

one can close the eyes and see that darkness is written on
    fleshy veils

the fibrous tunic that wraps one in white binds death close

that a breathing corpse might dwell within a word

that a word structures the body's bony labyrinths

or that another word might dwell within that word

and swallow that word wholly

OF APOCALYPSE

After that splendid flash had singed our shadows
to the walls of our apartments, painted the ashes
our bodies had become to brick, the Platonisms
we espoused seemed as perfunctory as the angel
figurines of nursing homes. In truth,
what surprised us was our souls living on,
for we had not anticipated the riotous failure
of our theologies. Eternity manifested more
a mall than a great cloud of unknowing. Agog,
we saw we had not so much left a cave
as we had a cinema, now passed through
some topiaried purgatory where the unassuming
wore crumpled tuxedos and ate moist cheeses.
No garden awaited us. Instead, we lumbered
into a rotunda of neon where fryers stood ready
to gild forgeries of those ersatz delicacies
we so eagerly enjoyed when we were corporeal.
With the help of escalators, ascension
was more or less a mechanical law
we simply had to submit to. We arose
stiff-legged into lofts of soft discounts,
marveled at the confidence of mannequins,
which seemed to resemble neighbors we once knew.
After hours of meandering, we were beckoned
to tables, and we sat, our trays rigid with
the faint aromas of—not our hunger, but the idea
of our needing to be hungry. And there,
in the fuzz of our anticipation, the rapture
of our honeyed boredom turned us
toward toasting. It was there, I recall,
that we, glistening in the cafeteria's

contoured warmth, our champagne flutes
raised to the muzak of the corridors,
became worthy of the disaster that had,
we believed, so suddenly taken us.

A PRAYER

as a voice turned out of its speech
a silence warm in my throat

a silence of cloth
clothed air

closed thought
to stitch out error

with a precise vowel
an opening

as to say O
and though I speak I

don't know what sound is sound
a damp mantle

over the teeth
slim sense

tucked in the breath
a seam in the tongue

a sentence
of death to speak

the divine
"God" at the center

a hole opens
the hole in

the idea of God
the idea of God

a round hum
an absence hymned as

O though I say I
don't know

to whom I say what
I say (what's said)

I might say O
my soul relinquish

this breath
behind the word

might ask what wind
whittles the voice

a thread
of its unsaid

underside
the strings of speech

knotted with knowing
or so I say O

is a thought wrapped
about the voice's hollow

hallowed though
I am not

still I breathe
I speak gaping

into that dark
halo though I hear

that deity is shrouded
by the prayer

swathed by breath
wronged in speech

though at its edges
some light lurks

some rapture slumps
through each sentence

so I say only
to say to oppose

all I am
though I say to know

myself as prayer
not said thing

a body bound
by voice

voice circled
in sound

I hear some echo
beneath each thing

feel the need
to slough speech

of the spoken
my voice within

its caverns
made absent

for some belief
as to what might

be there O
there O

(PSALM)

part self, part song

the psalm drags sense from absence

the eclogue anticipates response

verdant and vined, its verges

overtake the tongue, the daffodils'

yellow tolls silent

notes through the wind's sway,

blown and blasting

what diminishes

the leaf, blights the bright bloom

GOSPEL

The sky abrades, redacts a field with snow, lingers in.
Through the grey, the wind parses, pulls back the sheet

of storm, and houses blur into sight, boxy questions
the land can't answer. If there is a faith found in places

disowned by migrating geese, college boys, in barns
choked with rusted tools and rot-groomed timbers, it is not

one of return. As much as there is, there is also nothing.
A creek's cold water skates beneath ice, spills slow

over bottom stones. Silos fill distance between
earth and atmosphere, the cylinders tall with the heavy

knocks hammered through their steel. In a town
quilted by crops, barren pastures litter a traveler's

road in this late season. Every animal laid to rest
or slaughtered. Every traveler pauses, feels the bone

stiffen in the slendered air. But there are
no travelers. None. Homes divide into rooms

wide with creaking, tabled books open into stories
bare as the tombs at their end. From dark sleep's dark

waking, gowned forms rouse, stir, spark their candles,
and wait until the flames flicker, wicks spit as the tallow

melts into the warmth the sun easterly unlatches.
But what promise to wake into morning's absent latitude.

What comfort is daylight to we who are abandoned.

3

RUMINANT

You give the child a book.

There is sunlight, but first
the idea of sunlight.

warmth or *now*

You give the child a book
and a sentence

etches its length
into the hand.

Before the punctuation, a small
wren perched.

The child finds it

mute, unsung.

You give the child a book
and in it, a story.

Two sheep. A meadow.
A wolf. Red

appears as the color

of reading the story's
ending. The story ends

with a sudden violence.
And in this book, in this story,

the child finds
deep within the sheep

their stomachs gorged
with notes, hymnals

poised with noiselessness.

The child reads *psalterium*.

And what one thing is, it is.

Then the metaphors
leak too wide.

The child reads, *we are all sheep, we are
but grass.* In the story, the child

sees the paradox of praying, being
preyed upon.

An idea of

a small wren
nested in the O

of song

then flutters through the mind.

A simple thought

swaddled in the woolly
cloud of its language

becomes the woolly cloud.

You give the child a book,
and the child opens the book.

THE PARABLE'S PSALM

And for want of muscle slick under skin, spurs
of light on the tail's whip,
                    I creased my breath

into a vowel's pocket, hummed what hymns I knew
and sounded no more.
                    Then what landscape there was
was in my eye, my mouth a boon of grass, bent
or crushed.
            And into what was
        I went—

                    a valley chipped down to brush,
the hoofs green-shook it green.

                        That I stepped
into that force, beckoned *come, come.*

                        But that I saw the horses

bell into their neighs, nostrils waking, worried,
a storm thick in their flanks.

                    I said no more, and saw

their forms a thud of brown, black, their stampede,
        until what I said tore open,

some open book tore, its pages strewn.

(PSALM)

something like grace cottons the
brain when what's lost is lost. lambs

without shepherd huddle
a hill, eat their names

like tender shoots, as above
swallows feast in flight.

the air forked and feathered
with oscine frenzy, punctured

adjectives, draining. that whole field,
a cathexis of green, these

lambs the pasture
hearing what might be heard.

HYMN

        as into letters

dark winds turn

a page   that blow known

by leaves

   shaking

    the branch   the bud

broken   behind a pane

a sight   chiseled
of air   (the eye and its awl)
          (the ear and its conch)

the sound behind the bush's sound
the sound I say

to hear   (a purse of crickets)

to write to hear   to know   I am

aghast   gusted

against my speaking
the chirping   the chime

FABLE

we had to pull the bones from the birds to build their songs

our stomachs then a soak of feathers
our stomachs a bother of drowned hatchlings

we had to build their songs to find their stories

we had to tan their skins to form a page with music
  in its margins

those pages stitched with moth silk
those pages bound and sold

we were sorry to set so many words into currency

to place a tin cup in the mouth and fill it with coins
to cinch the mouth tight as a purse of coins

how all of our days our heads pecked with a tempo of beaks
how our cavities tumefied with terrible strains

INTERCESSORY

A Monday bound with bad
weather, nothing

but the stare of
the fog's flat color,
against which the street

shakes out
its wet coat.

I look out into it as if
searching for a light

gripped by oak
boughs, a light
muttered through

dumb clouds and their
logics of thunder.

But there isn't a body there.
There's no voice, no words

plowing through the
absence of their wakes.

But tiny boats on the sound.
Sailboats. Tones, ship-shaped.

In the frozen air, what I say
foregrounds me, shivers

what I might see. I walk
through a frosted ghost, the

mind retreats, memory
bending sight to its lens.

EVANGEL

What one considers endurance another considers patience,
        homologues
    rationed from their quaint particulars: either the whip's

lick or lash. If this is about love, you need a new dialectic
        consisting
    of flesh and dirt. If this is a heresy, there are no wounds

to touch. In an upper room, bread swims through wine,
        allocates
    betrayal's new language to a kiss. And there's

water for feet, wings beat against a window, a cup passes
    from one hand to the next. After, breath pleats

in your folded hands, a god answers its own petitions in a
        garden as the earth
    lumbers through its axial waltz. East and West contract

before you, the gloaming rims your iris's aperture. At another
    tomb, the lymph that spasms and bathes the tissue
        of a cloth-

bound body even stops the angels' tongues. Some time later,
        you find
    yourself in a new exemplum, waiting in a clean room's

corner. You tend the lamps. Inside a story a donkey brays,
        then speaks. Turn toward
    that wonder. Outside, rain quenches its sky. As if poured

from the moon's salted throat, the stars pock and glaze against
    it. You wander
  into that night as you would into a fable about night,

your lamp slaking the flame's thirst for kerosene's aliphatic
    brocade,
  its black wick long against the burn.

OTHER PSALMS

i.

Confession: I am a liar leaning into his fictions. The dawn an indifferent tableau. Such light. I am recalcitrant to distinguish it as bruised or brushed. Likewise, I am ignorant of seraphic conversations before coffee, though I am inclined to assume the sun is Isaiah's coal impressed then lifted from the earth's mouth, and therefore take every sprig and sprout as divine conjecture, a foretelling that grows into its elaboration.

ii.

When I tell you I do not have a prayer, you must side with the literal
or ironic. There are certain silences that haunt the body's bellows.
This is not to say prayer necessitates language. All at once, silence
conjugates. A mouth speaks, and it is not illogical to assume the
word is the self's antecedent, which is also to say silence has certain
consequences. There are reasons to believe metaphor is problematic
for reasoning, which is to say I do not have a prayer.

iii.

Silence swells with the noise of listening. A still, small voice scabs the ear.

iv.

Tulips and daffodils fastidious in their sapping of soil. Robins in their toil and worm-tug. The sizzle of yolks and whites in the pan. Other hasty emergences as troubled resurrections. Praise God, for there is a miracle in the meal, though it is admittedly one-sided. Praise God, for in the beginning a voice said *let there be* and darkness was untied from its dense collapse.

v.

But there was still darkness.

vi.

Confession: I am inclined to read myself into texts. The scriptures
rife with contradictions, nonetheless: beautiful multiplicities. A
burning wheel or Ezekiel's angels in jackets of eyes. When reading
the prophets, when speaking of transcendence, I assume there are
riddles the bones pose for the body. I imagine my scapula as the evo-
lutionary promise of wings or as the fossils of their loss. When read-
ing of miracles, I consider the vast migrations occurring beneath the
skin's tent. I consider the hypothesis: the body's systemized network
of electrical impulse is nothing short of miraculous, but it is not the
miracle. I consider: do not consider the system; consider its traffic.

vii.

Confession: when writing or praying, I have no idea what I am doing, or to whom I speak. I do not find this problematic as of yet. There are precise joys to spring. Aromatic draughts pinched in herbs, for instance. Rain, petrichor. Aubades and serenades, but, alas, the noon remains uptight without its odes.

viii.

The dusk similar to a book's closing or the impatience one discovers at the book's end. When I contemplate ecstatic vision, it is not difficult to imagine the sky red with apocalypse. I await the angel muzzling its lips to the horn. But there are swifter revelations, subtler incarnations. There is the desire to distill the nocturne's harmonics to the fissures of the crickets' supple congregations. I imagine that music black with pitch. All at once, various elisions occur.

ix.

Let me begin by saying the prophet's name was Nathan, the psalmist was a king, which is not in the least coincidental. I am still inclined to imagine the sun a coal impressed upon the earth's mouth. Let me begin by saying, all at once the night erupts as the condensation of a particular flower's aroma. I do not withhold the possibility of saying a lily, but I do not say *lily*.

4

THE SAME OLD STORY

Of course the expected, the beginning.

The narrator concludes that each word is a landscape and drinks the lake of its vowels.

The first utterance calls attention not to the text, but to the distance voice spans.

The narrator does not know this.

The narrator fashions every *he* and *she* and *it* as image.

Because all writing is formal, the narrator proceeds with courtesy.

Because most meaning is accidental, the narrator feigns intention.

As the story progresses, the voice grows faint, absorbed by each sentence.

The characters fall into the dark ink of their persons and call it transgression.

They plunge into metaphor if only to be carried across some great divide.

Their caresses are akin to reading—another knows another by the other form's warmth.

Now estranged in the narrative, the characters create conflict.

Now bloodied and sullen, the characters snug themselves
in the pouches of parentheses.

At the end of it, the narrator returns and finds its person
the cynosure of the story.

At its end, the narrator is speechless.

The characters have nothing left to say but what they
have said.

But they say anyway.

They say for the saying.

THE TRANSFIGURATION

the eye observes a canticle scored in the joint of a bee's wing

hears the turn of color bore a hive, honey-drunk

or the ear tunes its sight by vibration

the jar and hustle of molecules funneled until the incarnation
of bone-lilt

trouble begins when the divine tropes

an untethered tenor devoid suitable vehicle

there language flexes even image's paratactic wall

bee or bird cannot adequately signify the logarithms that pun
gravity

the poem mulls the dreams of sap spooled in wood despite
that pith's lack of prattle

even in verse, something like religion burgeons beneath
the surface

pathetic as all fallacies, willows and dove do what they will

light catches in a pane of glass and transubstantiates vision,
a glare

there: a voice thrown into a void where each word treads

like a new moon on a midnight lake

teased out, the song remains true to its falsities

satisfied to cradle divinity by flutter or buzz

and there: a voice recalls the ascetic whose body is a vaulted
   speck of earth

the ears poise

the eyes saccade beneath their lids

THE TALK

that what lord is
is not what is
was when is was
an in in us
was not an or
or an else that
was the some of
us was a small
is but not the
is that knows what
lord is not the
is that is the
late was not the
was that knows what
lord is but that
is that is its
is is that what
lord is who would
know not us not
the is or else
or or in lord
not is or was
not that none know
no not that what
lord is is not
but is its is
is what is it

BESTIARY

the parable of the fox is not a parable of den

the parable of the blackbird is not a parable

the tuft of fur in the bramble betrays flight

and the pinion in the bush is an archaic pen

further off, a storm hunches, silently

the wind's teeth fall from its mouth, quietly

in this parable, when the rain falls, the copse is an open hand

when the moon rises, the stars are its argument

in this parable, sight stops after a great distance

under its seeming, the hounds woof through the thicket

inside their baying, the fox is a bloodied pelt in their jaws

then the blackbird is a small letter when it flies

or the flock at the horizon does not reach its east

in this parable, plot is perimeter

and escape scurries and hides

when we read this parable, a sky littered with periods is all
we see

a starved animal slinks into the body and sleeps there

THE SHEPHERD'S SONG

for want of white I slew a lamb
for want of warmth I wore him

for with a blow air cleaves with bleat
for want is the trough loss spills in

OF REVELATION

Consider emphysema's elegance
when you hear that in youth he snuck
behind a rock wall, his body a pocket
of breath. And there, in his lips,
a cigarette's slow char, a bone stripped
back to reveal the marrow's
chalked fire. The field spread with
the chaos of butterflies' flight,
and distantly, a church swabbed its bells clean.
But know this isn't a bucolic hymn,
though who doesn't want a slice
of Americana? Who doesn't want a name
like Arkansas? So the horses that pressed
that fence weren't horses, just
a sinewed memory of the West. So when it
first happens, he doesn't even feel it,
a catch of cells sing their mutinous freedom,
some echo smothers his alveoli.
In years, doctors will chart his body
by limb and joint, pulse and second while
he breathes. Only later, when carcinoma
barnacles his spine, when his lungs
bud tumors like so many bulbs
half-buried in soil, under tubes of florescent
gossip, will he swear he sees
God's face, threshed brightness, a broken light.

PSALM, STUNTED

The morning thick
with the thickness

of thick things. The
sky's flat pallet

grey. My windows
glossy with each new

Feathers culled
from holly, the wind

picking. One nest.
Yolks shelled in blue.

The day lost to

Some flight unbelievable.
I am not believing.

The birds fold and crash
into their glass songs.

The gust. The blow.

I cannot say I know what faint—

I cannot say I know

THE HERETIC

Bound as I was
to the empty

promises of
a scroll's archaic

glyphs, the ventilated
allegories of

gospels believed
to be written by

ghouls resurrected
by the backward

spells of so many
magicians, I

couldn't escape
the irony that

my martyrdom
would catalyze

devotion to
orthodoxies

as yet unheralded
and unknown. For

rather than rejoice
at the sting

of persecution,
what followers

conjuring a
stoic stand

from a terrified
body disemboweled

of breath will themselves rest
within the eye of a tempest

and believe its
pleasant drizzle

the unrelenting
torrent of a

principality
they had too long been

to realize they were?
And bound as I was

to the stake, I
had little recourse

but to retreat
into my discrete

visions, for as
my accusers read

me my heresy,
a prophecy pushed

through their clipped
reproaches like

the locust its chitin,
a new plot

gasped like
a lover arching

into ecstasy.
I then knew

that before the sky
would drape

the hills like
a shroud a corpse,

before those who
would don my

name like a gown
of station and

spend evenings
on rooftops believing

some god would
deliver them from

a world that was
the only home

heaven meant,
suited men, whose

silhouettes were
fabricated from

the shadows
of extinct species

poised in a diorama's
painted twilight,

would rise from
their sleep to watch

the sun appear
a coin plucked

from a pocket
by an invisible

hand. As they would
baptize it beautiful,

the end would come.
But yet after this

revelation, after
I saw the night

ripped from
its stiches of stars,

and, like a flag
flogged by wind,

tatter further
into flaying,

a curtain lifted
and the sea stilled.

Fathoms below
its absolute surface,

the last blue whale
intoned a desolate

song to nothing
but the mineral dark

until its melodies
beached on the shores

of each continent.
Floating face down

over bleached reefs,
the last tourist

heard it through
the clenched density

of packed water.
But before she could

puzzle its riddle,
the scene crumbled

like an antique page
brought too swiftly

into the stark day.
It was that last

vision the pop
of kindling and

snap of flames
dispelled. Only then,

as I choked on
smoke teased from

my blistering
skin, did I see

I was at the
heart of a world

that had long been
burning from

the inside out.

In the Permanent Collection, **by Stefanie Wortman**

"Intensity of heart, intensity of mind, flowering as one: Stefanie Wortman's poems redeem 'wit' back to its root meaning of 'insight' or 'vision,' the same root as the Sanskrit 'veda.' For example: the resonance of 'shades' when the words 'blind king' on a truck mean not Lear but 'installer of shades.' Or, a dance of death where the words 'trips' and 'plays' have doubled, heartbreaking and celebratory meanings. *In the Permanent Collection* merits its title."

—**Robert Pinsky**, author of *Gulf Music* and
1997–2000 U. S. Poet Laureate

"These poems seem haunted by a mostly nameless melancholia. *In the Permanent Collection,* however, turns its grim geography of prisons, mortuaries, and tawdry suburbs into something close to classical elegy. 'In sunken rooms,' Wortman writes, 'on scratchy rugs, maybe we've never known happiness.' It's that 'maybe'—the smart hedge—that renders her poems complex, often beguiling, but never without a gesture of redemption. This should be part of any serious poet's permanent collection."

—**Chad Davidson**, author of *The Last Predicta*

"In this gorgeous, self-possessed book, Stefanie Wortman doses out pleasure and pain in perfect measure, her symphonic formal skills setting us up for unexpected heartbreak. Wortman's poems look for redemption in and as art—and as such console even as they seek out consolation themselves. They are spirited and haunted, intimate and estranged. *In the Permanent Collection* is a first book by a poet who has already hit her stride."

—**Gabriel Fried**, author of *Making the New Lamb Take*

Club Icarus, **by Matt W. Miller**

"A down-to-earth intelligence and an acute alertness to the gritty movement of language are what you'll treasure most in Matt Miller's *Club Icarus.* You just might pass this book on to a friend or relative who needs it, or even better yet, purchase their own copy."

—**Major Jackson**, author of *Holding Company* and judge

"In Matt Miller's deeply satisfying collection, there is a visceral long-ing that cannot be ignored, a surrender to the body's fate but also a warring against it. There is the tenacious blood-grief for the lost father but also the deeply abiding yet fearful love of the new father. At the heart of these wonderful poems is a naked wrestling with all those forces that both wither life and give it bloom, those that rob us and those that save us."

—**Andre Dubus III**, author of *House of Sand and Fog*

"In a stunning array throughout Matt W. Miller's remarkable *Club Icarus* are instances of the kind of poetic alchemy that coaxes beauty and a rather severe grace out of the most obdurate materials and unlikely contexts. Here is a poet in whose artful hands language has become an instrument that enables us to know the world again and, simultaneously, as if for the first time."

—**B. H. Fairchild**, winner of the National Book Critics Circle Award for Poetry

"In *Club Icarus* the universal themes of birth and death, love and loss—are woven together with a luminous, transcendent brush. This book is a sly and beautiful performance."

—**Marilyn Chin**, author of *Rhapsody in Plain Yellow*

Death of a Ventriloquist, by Gibson Fay-LeBlanc

"Whether he's overhearing a conversation in a tavern or the music stuck in his head, Fay-LeBlanc uses his ventriloquist to raise import-ant questions about how we perform ourselves through language. The tension that permeates his poetry—what is seen and unseen, said and eavesdropped, true and trickery—culminates in a debut that rings out long after Fay-LeBlanc's lips stop moving."

—*Publishers Weekly* starred review

"What drives the poems in this wonderfully animated debut volume and prompts the reader's pleasure in them is the patent honesty of the poet's voice. In the 'ventriloquist' series itself, Fay-LeBlanc cre-ates a remarkable refracted self-portrait, bristling with moments of unabashed illumination."

—**Eamon Grennan**, author of *Out of Sight*

"In the words of visual artist Paul Klee, 'art doesn't reproduce what we can see, it makes it visible.' The turf of these poems is a 'vision country' in which our narrator / ventriloquist makes visible (and audible) the world to which he restlessly attends."

—**Lisa Russ Spaar**, author of *Satin Cash* and judge

"Gibson Fay-LeBlanc is a new poet with an old voice. The ventriloquist here throws his own voice while sitting on his own knee, speaking for, but not to, himself, making magic in (and of) plain sight."

—**Brenda Shaughnessy** author of *Human Dark with Sugar*

Circles Where the Head Should Be, by Caki Wilkinson

"Playful and soulful, buoyant and mordant, snazzy and savvy—Caki Wilkinson's poems pull out all the stops, and revel in making the old mother tongue sound like a bright young thing. Lend her your ears and you'll hear American lyric moxie in all its abounding gusto and lapidary glory, making itself new all over again."

—**David Barber**, Poetry Editor, *The Atlantic*

"*Circles Where the Head Should Be* has its own distinctive voice, a lively intelligence, insatiable curiosity, and a decided command of form. These qualities play off one another in ways that instruct and delight. An irresistible book."

—**J. D. McClatchy**, author of *Mercury Dressing: Poems,* judge

"Caki Wilkinson's marvelous and marvelously titled *Circles Where the Head Should Be* contains poetry as dexterously written as any today. And beneath its intricate surface pleasures lie a fierce intelligence and a relentless imagination constantly discovering connections where none had been seen before. This is a stunning debut."

—**John Koethe**, author of *Ninety-fifth Street,*
winner of the Lenore Marshall Prize

"Like Frost, Wilkinson believes in poem as performance, showing off her verve and virtuosity. She is the 'Lady on a Unicycle,' negotiating her difficult vehicle through the pedestrian crowd with 'the easy lean achieved/ by holding on to nothing'—a joy to witness."

—**A. E. Stallings**, author of *Archaic Smile* and *Hapax*

Stray Home, by Amy M. Clark:

Two poems from *Stray Home* were selected by Garrison Keillor, host of *A Prairie Home Companion* and of *The Writer's Almanac,* to be included in *The Writer's Almanac,* broadcast May 28 and 29, 2010.

"*Stray Home* is a great read. The poetic form found in its pages never feels forced or full of clichés. Whether you are a fan of formal verse or just like to 'dabble,' *Stray Home* is a collection to pick up."

—*Good Reads*

Ohio Violence, by Alison Stine:

"In the mind, Ohio and violence may not be words immediately paired—pastoral cornfields, football fields, and deer versus the blood and splintered bone of a fight or a death. Yet *Ohio Violence* achieves that balance of the smooth and vivid simmer of images and the losses that mount in Alison Stine's collection."

—*Mid-American Review*

"Shot through with a keen resolve, *Ohio Violence* is an arresting, despairing book that alternately stuns and seduces."

—*Rain Taxi*

"One comes away from *Ohio Violence* newly impressed with the contingency and instability of the hazardous universe that is our home; and impressed, as well, with the ability of these stark, memorable poems to distill that universe into language and to make of it a sad and haunting song."

—**Troy Jollimore**, *Galatea Resurrects #13*

Mister Martini, by Richard Carr:

"This is a truly original book. There's nothing extra: sharp and clear and astonishing. Viva!"

—**Naomi Shihab Nye**, author of *Fuel,* judge

The Next Settlement, by Michael Robins:

"Michael Robins' prismatic poems open windows, then close them, so we're always getting glimpses of light that suggest a larger world.

With never a syllable to spare, these poems are beautiful and haunting. I know of nothing like them."

—**James Tate**, winner of the 1992 Pulitzer Prize for Poetry

"*The Next Settlement* is a finely honed, resonant collection of poems, sharp and vivid in language, uncompromising in judgment. The voice in this book is unsparing, often distressed, and involved in a world which is intrusive, violent, and deeply deceitful, where honesty and compassion are sought for in vain, and refuges for the mind are rare."

—**Anne Winters**, author of *The Key to the City*, judge

re-entry, **by Michael White:**

"Michael White's third volume does what all good poetry does: it presents the sun-drenched quotidiana of our lives, and lifts it all into the sacred space of poetry and memory. He delights us with his naming, but he also makes us pause, long enough at least to take very careful stock of what we have. He makes us want to hold on to it, even as it trembles in the ether and dissolves."

—**Paul Mariani**, author of *Deaths and Transfigurations*, judge

"Here is a book that explores the interplay between interior and exterior landscapes with such generous and beautifully crafted detail that readers will feel they are no longer reading these poems but living them."

—**Kathryn Stripling Byer**, Poet Laureate
of North Carolina 2005–2009

"In Michael White's latest opus, figure after figure emerge from chaotic ground of memory, such verdant upswellings an urgent music pressured up from deep wells before subsiding—high waterlines left in our wake to mark the turbulence of love's intractable flood."

—**Timothy Liu**, author of *For Dust Thou Art*

CPSIA information can be obtained at www.ICGtesting.com
Printed in the USA
LVOW09s0006200215

427622LV00003B/18/P